SOUTH SUSSEX WALKS

The numbered arrow points to the start of each walk

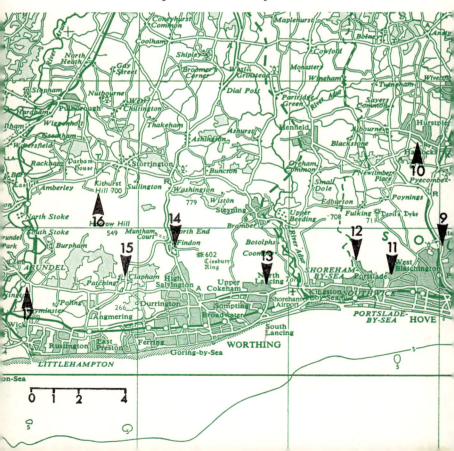

BBC Radio Brighton

South Sussex Walks

Lord Teviot
in collaboration with
Michael B. Quinion

British Broadcasting Corporation

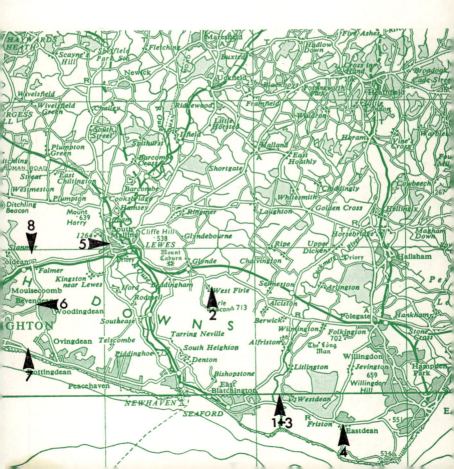

Published by the British Broadcasting Corporation
35 Marylebone High Street, London W1M 4AA

SBN 563 09364 1

First Published 1970
Reprinted 1970 and 1972

© *Lord Teviot and Michael B. Quinion 1970*

Printed in England by
Ebenezer Baylis & Son Limited
The Trinity Press
Worcester, and London

Contents

1: Westdean Circular *page* 9
*Westdean Corner - Hobb's Hawth – Alfriston – Litlington – Westdean
Corner*
10 miles; downland, river and woodland; refreshments at 7 and 8 miles;
easy.

2: Old Coach Road Circular 12
*Firle Village – The Old Coach Road – Bopeep – Alfriston – Firle Beacon –
Firle Village*
10 miles; weald and downland; refreshments halfway; one steep climb.

3: Seven Sisters Circular 14
*Westdean Corner – Friston Forest – Eastdean – Birling Gap – Seven
Sisters – Cuckmere Haven – Westdean Corner*
8 or 10 miles; woods, downland, river and cliffs; refreshments halfway
on longer version; many small hills.

4: Eastdean Circular 18
Eastdean – Birling Gap – Crowlink – Friston Corner – Eastdean
4½ miles; downs and cliffs; no refreshments on route; a few hills.

5: Lewes Circular 19
*Lewes – Mount Harry – Blackcap – Newmarket Inn – Newmarket Hill –
Jugg's Road – Kingston – Lewes*
12 miles; all downland; refreshments halfway; easy.

6: Woodingdean Circular 20
*Woodingdean – Balsdean – Highdole Hill – Rodmell – Jugg's Road –
Woodingdean*
6, 10 or 12 miles; all downland; refreshments only on longest version;
easy, but many hills.

7: Roedean Circular 23
Roedean – Ovingdean – Woodingdean – Roedean
4½ miles; all downland; refreshments halfway; easy.

8: Falmer Circular 24
*Falmer – St Mary's Farm – Streathill Farm – Buckland Bank – Waterpit
Hill – Falmer*
4½ miles downland, with wealden views; no refreshments on route;
easy.

9: Patcham to Stanmer 27
Patcham – The Chattri – Ditchling Beacon – Stanmer Park
7 miles; downland; refreshments at start and end; easy.

10: Hurstpierpoint to Patcham 29
Hurstpierpoint – Danny Park – Wolstonbury Hill – Pyecombe – Sweet Hill – Patcham
7 miles; weald and downs; refreshments after 5 miles; steep climb at one point.

11: Hangleton Circular 32
Hangleton – Devil's Dyke – Fulking Hill – Foredown Hospital – Hangleton
$7\frac{1}{2}$ miles; downland with wealden views; refreshments halfway; easy.

12: Mile Oak Circular 34
Mile Oak – Edburton Hill – Truleigh Hill – Beeding Hill – Thundersbarrow Hill – Mile Oak
7 miles; downland with wealden views; no refreshments on route; easy.

13: North Lancing Circular 36
North Lancing – Steep Down – Cissbury Ring – Chanctonbury Ring – Coombes – North Lancing
11 to 14 miles; downland; refreshments by detour to Findon only; easy but long.

14: Findon Circular 40
Findon – Sullington – Washington – Chanctonbury Ring – Findon
9 miles; downland and weald; refreshments halfway; one steep climb.

15: Patching Woods Circular 42
$7\frac{1}{2}$ miles; woods and a little downland; no refreshments; easy.

16: Parham Post Circular 45
Parham Post – Amberley – North Stoke – Burpham – Wepham Down – Parham Post
9 miles; downland, wealden views and river; refreshments after 2 and $4\frac{1}{2}$ miles; easy.

17: Arundel to Goring 47
Arundel – Lyminster – Poling – Angmering – Goring
$7\frac{1}{2}$ miles; coastal plain and downland; refreshments after 4 miles; easy.

Introduction

The origin of this little book is curious. Some years ago my wife and I, feeling the need of fresh air and exercise, began to walk in the country. Our small, lively Jack Russell bitch has always been absolutely tireless, and has spurred us on to venture further and further afield. Other interests sprang from our walks, like visiting old churches, and archaeology, which I must confess I still know little about, but which I find absolutely fascinating. Early in 1968, just after the inauguration of BBC Radio Brighton, I was approached by Mike Matthews, the then producer of 'The Countryside Hereabouts', to broadcast a series of rambles. His successor, Michael Quinion, invited me to do a second series the following year. These happily produced a very encouraging response from listeners, many of whom took the trouble to obtain the broadsheets he wrote out describing the walks. I know that many house-bound people also liked to listen to my descriptions, as they have brought back nostalgic memories. Hence the idea of this publication was born. Michael Quinion offered to act as watchdog-in-chief, which he has done with a meticulous and ruthless thoroughness, as well as having walked most of the rambles. This book has not been produced specifically for the experienced rambler, though I trust even he or she will find it a useful guide. There are, in fact, a tremendous number of other people who are extremely keen on getting out into the country and walking, but who are hesitant to do so because they don't know where to begin for various reasons. The main one being that they aren't sure of the rights of way and fear they might be trespassing. Signposting is improving, owing to the statutory requirements of the Country-side Act 1968, but it still has a long way to go, and even when paths are signposted, it doesn't necessarily follow that they are passable. There are many that have become overgrown and obstructed through lack of use. Thus, we have done our best to thoroughly check that all these ways are in a reasonable condition. One cannot guarantee more, because at certain times of the year (especially before hay-making) fields become overgrown, and some paths, as I'm sure you all know, become very muddy in wet weather. The area that we have chosen for walking is from the coast at Eastdean, in East Sussex, to the Arun River in West Sussex, taking in all the downland between these two points and going into the Weald a short way. Unfortunately, we have not been able to cover all the ground within these boundaries in this publication; for example, we have had to leave out any mention of Telscombe. In order to suit the convenience of the majority of people we have made most of the rambles circular, and great attention has been paid to both car-parking and public transport facilities. There are, however, three that can only practically be carried out by train or bus. As bus routes and times vary from season to season, we have contented ourselves with giving you general information about bus routes. Up-to-date details can be had from the bus companies' offices. We have included maps of the area of each walk (they are reduced by about a tenth from the black printing of the one-inch ordnance survey sheets – the grid is of kilometre squares), to give you an idea of the country, but we think the instructions are adequate even without the maps. You might like to have your own maps as an extra guide. The one-inch Ordnance Survey Maps 182 and 183 cover the area, but if you acquire the two-and-a-half-inch maps, they will naturally give you more detail. These walks have wherever possible been designed to provide an opportunity for refreshments at some suitable halfway point. As nearly all the walks are circulars it is quite possible to begin them at some intermediate point but usually this plays havoc with the refreshments. We have also tried to indicate points of interest along the route. If you want to find out more about the churches, country houses and so on which are mentioned, I suggest that *Sussex* in the Buildings of England Series by Pevsner (Penguin), *Along the South Downs* by David Harrison (Cassell) and *Sussex* in the Kings England Series by Arthur Mee are useful books to have.

Our special thanks must go to James Rammell, a former Conservator of Forests in Kenya, who has undertaken the job of erecting several hundred wooden signposts marking rights of way within the West Sussex County area. This, by itself, would put him in the debt of every walker in the area, but he has also given us much practical advice and encouragement. Our thanks must go also to all the other people who have given us advice and help. Finally we do hope this book will become a friend and guide, and that you'll enjoy reading and using it as much as Michael Quinion and I have enjoyed compiling it.

Hove, Sussex,   *Teviot*
December 1969

8

General Description Westdean can be counted as one of the most unspoilt villages in Sussex. Until the Forestry Commission built houses for their staff, there had been little or no building for at least 150 years. It is practically certain that Alfred the Great owned a manor here. Just over the hill is Exceat, which now only consists of a farm and the bridge, but which was once a village of some size; it was wiped out in the Black Death in 1349. I apologise for making you suffer the A259 for a short way, but there is an adequate path beside it. When you leave the main road, you plunge deeper and deeper into the Downs along the Comp, and turn off just before the Five Lords Burghs, so named as five manors once met there. In the fields you will note round barrows, which were said to house the burial places of ancient kings – we now know they are indeed burial sites, dating from the Middle Bronze Age, but not, regretfully, of kings. You stay on the Downs until you plunge steeply into Alfriston, a village of great antiquity and once notorious for its smuggling activities. You cannot but notice the church, better known locally as the Cathedral of the Downs. You then have a peaceful quiet flat walk by the River Cuckmere, a river of great charm, as far as Litlington, where you cut across to Westdean, passing Charlston Manor, which is said to have been given to the cupbearer of Earl Warrenne, the son-in-law of William the Conqueror.

How to Get There By car, drive out on the A259. Westdean Corner is about ¼ mile east of Exceat Bridge, over the River Cuckmere. Turn off the main road, up the lane leading to Westdean, and park on the grass verge, just a few yards in. If you are travelling by bus, there is no need to do the first part of this walk. Catch a Southdown Bus Number 12 to Chyngton Lane, which is at the top of the hill on the Seaford side of the river, and pick up the directions from there.

Maps Since you would need no less than three sheets of the Ordnance Survey two-and-a-half-inch Map to cover this walk (Sheets TQ 40, TQ 50, TV 59), I suggest you take the one-inch Sheet 183 (Eastbourne) if you want to take a map at all. See our map on page 11.

Stage One: Westdean Corner to Alfriston – 7 miles Turn right, back on to the main road, and walk down it, over the river. Keep to the right-hand side going up the hill – there is a path, behind a low mound. At the top of the hill, turn right into Chyngton Lane North. At the point where the road bears right, to go up to Dymock Farm, keep straight on up the track in front of you. Follow the fence on the right for one mile – don't bear left on any of the paths leading into the houses.

Cross the Seaford to Alfriston Road and walk up the track opposite. It soon becomes completely unfenced and winds across the open downland for about $1\frac{1}{4}$ miles. You will come to some rough scrubland where the track disappears at the corner of a field but a few feet to the right a grass path leads between hedges in the same general direction. After a while you will pass the golf course on your left. Don't take the right fork at the end of the first section of the course but keep along the ridge. After another $\frac{3}{4}$ mile, your path runs into another (more clearly marked) path at a steep angle, making a triangular open space.

At this junction you should turn sharp right, through a small gate, and follow the track down into the valley and up the other side to a gate near the crest of the Downs. Go through this. Just before the ridge you will see your own track bending round to the left, to meet up with the South Downs Way, which you can see climbing the hill ahead of you. Turn right here, cutting the corner if you like, into the South Downs Way and walk along the edge of the scarp face of the Downs with the Weald on your left. After a little while you will go through a double gate. Turn left along the fence and follow the new track for $1\frac{1}{4}$ miles. Go through a metal gate and turn left. You will see Alfriston stretched out below you. After 100 yards leave the track, as it curves round to the left, and go steeply downhill along a grass track under some trees. This path leads into the top end of a road. Follow this down, past the school, into the village, turning right at the T-junction. This is an excellent place to break your journey as there is a café and a pub (The Market Cross Inn) which serves snacks and which has a restaurant.

Stage Two: Alfriston to Westdean Corner – 3 miles Take the turning off the main road, nearly opposite the Market Cross Inn. Walk down to the river and turn right. Cross the footbridge, and walk down the left bank, over three fences, until you come to some trees on the left. Walk past them for a few yards and just before the next footbridge turn left into the trees along a narrow tarmac path. Turn right into the main road, passing The Plough

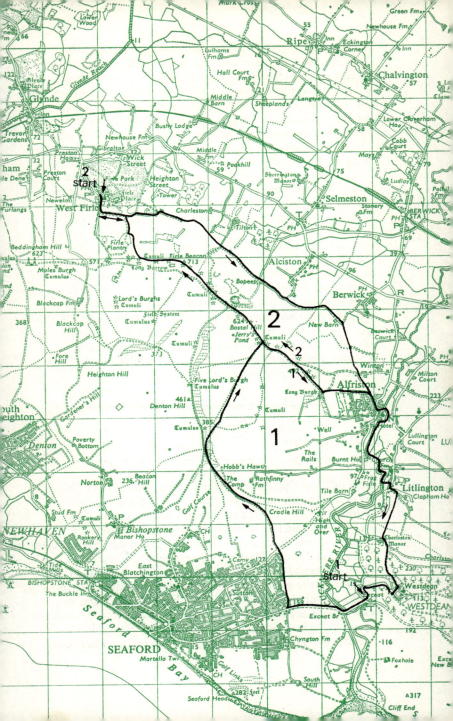

and Harrow. Seventy-five yards further on turn left into a lane – there's a board at the entrance saying 'private road to Clapham House'. Twenty yards up the lane turn right through a gap in the hedge, and through a stile. Follow the path across the field and up the hill. Go under some overgrown hawthorn bushes, and keep left along the side of the field. In the far corner go over a fence, and through a gate, to follow the line of the fence on the same side as before. Go through another gate into a fourth field. Keep just to the right of the fence down into the valley. Go through a wire gate in the corner and turn left round the edge of the trees. After 150 yards turn right up the steep slope. At the top of the hill you will come out in one of the rides of Friston Forest. Follow the line of the electricity poles along the rides for about half a mile. You will come to a narrower, rougher ride which you should follow to its end at some chestnut fencing. Walk down the narrow path at the side of the fencing, across the entrance to the cottage, and along a grass path marked by white stones into the trees again. Turn right down the concrete-paved track to the road. Turn half-right into it, and go down to the junction at the bottom. Cross the road and go up the lane by the telephone box. A few yards up turn right through a gate into another ride. Walk down it, following it as it bears to the left. This will bring you out on the main road at Westdean Corner. To catch a bus from here turn left and go round the corner – you will find a bus stop opposite the farm entrance.

---

2 *Firle Village – The Old Coach Road – Bopeep – Alfriston – Firle Beacon – Firle Village*   10 miles

---

General Description Most people, I imagine, think of Firle as the cause of an uncomfortably sharp bend in the Lewes to Eastbourne road. Few bother to explore this very attractive village, which has been in the hands of the Gage family for well over four hundred years – the church is full of brasses and memorials to them. At the far end of the village you come to the Old Coach Road, which passes under the Downs – completely unaltered and untouched. In the winter it becomes extremely muddy, which in itself is a reminder of what roads were like in bygone days. As you walk along, you pass the lonely Beanstalk – two cottages, numbered 84 and 85 – where Numbers 1 to 83 can be, I can't possibly imagine. Later on, you come to Bopeep, where there was once a

coaching inn, called The Half Moon; it is now a private house –
curiously enough, it has a solicitor's plate outside.

While walking along you can't help but become engrossed in the
past. On grey winter's days, I sometimes imagine I can almost hear
the sound of the horses' hooves, the creaking of the carriage wheels
and the jingle of the harness.

On your return over the Downs from Alfriston you must look out
for the church spires of Berwick, Alciston, Selmeston, Ripe, and
Chalvington in the weald below you. Just a little way past the
gliding station, on Firle Beacon, you come back down to Firle by
way of the Plantation.

To Get to Firle If you're coming by bus take Southdown Service
25, which runs from Brighton to Eastbourne via Lewes, and get off
at Firle Corner. By train, get off at Glynde Station and walk down
to Firle – about 1½ miles away. If you come by car turn off the A27
at Firle Corner, about 3 miles east of Lewes, and park in the village.

Maps The most convenient map is the Ordnance Survey one-
inch Sheet 183 (Eastbourne). It gives enough detail to trace out
the walk easily. If you want to use the two-and-a-half-inch sheets,
the Numbers are TQ 40 and TQ 50. See also our map on page 11.

Stage One: Firle Village to Alfriston – 5 miles Walk down the
lane, from Firle Corner, bearing left at the fork. Walk through the
village, past the Ram Inn, to the end of the road. You will find the
Home Farm on the left, by a lane leading to the Church and Firle
Place. Keep straight on, following the sign saying 'Bridle Way
Only', past the entrance to the farm and through a gate. After
250 yards, follow the track round to the left, close to the wall.
After a ¼ mile the track forks – again follow the wall to the left. After
200 yards, your track disappears through a gateway on the left – do
not follow it, but keep straight ahead along the grassy track.

A little way further on you run into a track coming from a field on the
right. Bear left, past those two oddly-numbered cottages I mentioned, and immediately right again on to the line of the path. You
will go round the edge of a couple of fields after which the track
narrows to a path on the right-hand side of a wire fence beside
some trees. After a while the track widens again, but becomes a
little overgrown, though it can still be followed. In the next little
valley you pick up a chalk track coming in from the left. Follow
this to a group of buildings and take the left fork at the cottage.
This takes you to a metal gate, giving access to a made-up road,
which leads to the gliding station. The house here is Bopeep. Cross
the road, and go down the path to the left of the house.

About 1½ miles further on you will pass a barn on the right. When you are almost opposite Berwick Church – a spire above some trees to the left – the track bears round towards it. Don't follow it, but turn off half-right along a narrow path under some trees. You will come out at a junction, on the corner of a lane. Walk straight down the small hill in front of you into Alfriston. There's a pub (The Market Cross Inn) and a café.

Stage Two: Alfriston back to Firle – 5 miles On coming out of the pub, turn left back up the lane you came down. Turn left into a concrete-paved road, past some houses and a school, to the end of the road. Continue up the steep hill, along the path through the trees. Near the top of the hill bear left into a main track. After 100 yards turn right through a metal gate.

Walk along the ridge of the Downs for 1¼ miles. Then turn half-right through a double gate and continue along the Downs. You will go down into a dip, through two gates, and past the hangar of the gliding station. On the crest of the next hill, Firle Beacon, you will pass an Ordnance Survey Triangulation Pillar on your right. Go through the big gate at the end of this field – not the small one in the right-hand corner. On the other side follow the less clearly marked track slightly to the right and after 200 yards bear further right, over to the fence, and follow it down into the dip. The faint path becomes a proper track, and leads you downhill to the edge of a plantation. Go through the small gate. Once inside the field walk down the right-hand side of the trees at the edge of the field to the *second* gate, and go into the plantation. Just inside the trees turn right on to the track leading downhill. This brings you out on the Coach Road again. Turn left and walk back along the track, past the Home Farm, into Firle village.

3 *Westdean Corner – Friston Forest – Eastdean – Birling Gap – Seven Sisters – Cuckmere Haven – Westdean Corner* 8 or 10 miles

General Description Once again you start at Westdean, which I have described in the introduction to Walk 1, although I didn't mention the church, which has unusual and interesting monuments inside, including an Epstein bust, as well as a Norman bell-tower. The priest house, next to the church, is reported to be one of the oldest inhabited houses in Sussex.

Friston Forest is extremely fine. It is run by the Forestry Commission, being their only holding of any size in the area. It is planted with a mixture of trees – you can obtain further details from the forester's hut by the entrance. The Commission have arranged a forest walk which you might like to do some time – once again, details can be got from the hut. If I'm likely to get lost anywhere, it's in a forest, but here you're walking on the main track, so I think you should be all right. You pass by Friston Place, a fine Tudor house, and the original house of the Selwyn family, now owned by Lord Shawcross, a former Attorney General. Further on you come to Friston Pond, and so down to Eastdean, which lies pleasantly in a hollow. This is a good place to stop because it has a fine old inn (The Tiger) and a nice green beside it. I've suggested a short-cut at one point to reduce the walk by 2 miles, but bear in mind that you miss Eastdean altogether by following it.

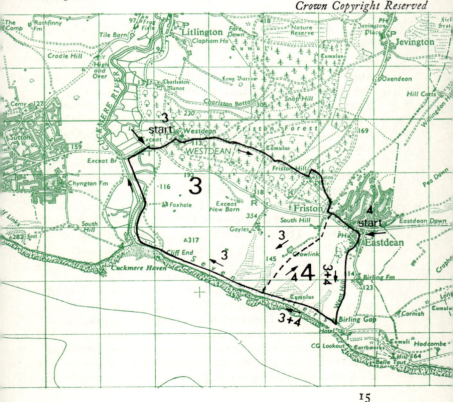

From Eastdean, you travel on over a pleasant stretch of downland to Birling Gap, and along the Seven Sisters to Cuckmere Haven. These Seven Sisters are in reality seven hills, falling steeply to the sea – you see them best from Seaford Head, on the other side of the Haven. They're all named: Haven Brow, Short Brow, Rough Brow, Brass Point, Flagstaff Point, Bailey's Hill, and Went Hill – a nice mixture of the romantic and the mundane. Once in the Haven you will follow the river bank up to Exceat Bridge, and so back to Westdean.

To get to Westdean Corner By bus, you should catch the Southdown Service 12 and get off at the stop round the corner, called Exceat Farm, a few yards away from the lane leading up to Westdean. By car, you should travel out on the A259 and turn up the lane, signposted to Westdean, about a $\frac{1}{4}$ mile on the Eastbourne side of Exceat Bridge. Park on the verge a few yards up. I suggest you don't try to park in the village itself – there's very little room available.

Maps Either use the one-inch Ordnance Survey Sheet 183 (Eastbourne) or the two-and-a-half-inch Sheet TV59 (Eastbourne). Our map is on page 15.

Stage One: Westdean Corner to Eastdean – 4 miles If you've come by car walk out on the main road, in the direction of Eastbourne, and walk round the bend in the road. Just opposite the bus stop there is a farm entrance. If you've come by bus you've been set down here. Turn into the farm entrance, through the five-barred gate in front of you, and straight up the hill. At the wall near the top you will find some stone steps conveniently placed. On the other side of the wall there is a well-trodden path that leads you steeply down the hill. You will come out by a telephone box on the road in Westdean village. Turn right, walk along the road for 300 yards, go round the corner to the left, and up the hill. Just where the road bends to the left again, there's a road off to the right, marked with (among others) the sign, 'Forestry Commission – Friston Forest'. Go up this road, past a pole-gate across it at the Forest Office, and along a chalk track straight ahead of you. You will pass a house on your left 200 yards on. A hundred yards past this house leave the ride and strike off half-right up a rough track, which brings you out into another ride parallel to the first. Keep going in the same direction as before for about a mile, down into the valley and up the other side. At the top of this hill (Friston Hill) the ride opens out into a wide grassy place. Keep by the trees on the right-hand side, pick up the ride on the other side, and go on down the hill. You will come out of the ride at a cross roads – Friston Place is ahead of you. Turn left into the lane, and turn right after 100 yards into another lane with the sign 'No Right of Way'. Just to reassure you, the lane is a public bridlepath – the Waterworks Department mean it's no right of way for vehicles.

About 150 yards up this lane you will see some glasshouses over the wall on the right, and, about a hundred yards ahead, a widening of the road on both sides to allow vehicles to pass. Halfway between these two there is an inconspicuous gate, set in the wall on the right, between bushes. Go through the gate into the field, and aim half-left for a similar gate in the wall on the other side – how visible the path is depends on the time of year. Go through the other gate, down the steps, across the drive, and over the stile into the field opposite. Follow the faint path diagonally up the hill to the top far corner, and into the trees by way of the stile. From here on the path is quite clear and brings you out through a five-barred gate on to the main road again, at Friston Corner. Cross the road to the bus shelter.

If you want to take the short-cut, jump here in the instructions to stage three. Otherwise, by the bus-shelter, you will find a green metal sign pointing out a narrow asphalt path. Follow this behind the trees, down the hill into Eastdean Village. If you walk down the road opposite you will find the Tiger Inn where you can get a snack.

Stage Two: Eastdean Village to Westdean Corner – 6 miles
Cross the Green from the Tiger Inn and go up Went Way, which is signposted 'No Through Road'. Go up this road to the end, over the stile, and follow the track round to the left for a few yards. Now strike off uphill along the track into the trees. There is a clear path through the trees which brings you out on to the open Down. Turn left, beside the bushes, towards the red-roofed barn. You will come across a beaten track, just to the right of the barn, leading down the other side of the hill. After 300 yards you will see a small gate ahead of you. Go through it, and down the path to the cliff-edge, past the bungalows on the left. Turn right at the pillar and go up the hill with the cliff-edge on your left. Go through the gate on to the National Trust property and follow the path at a safe distance from the cliff-edge over the Seven Sisters. Just keep going until you come to the edge of the steep hill overlooking Cuckmere Haven. Find your way down the very steep slope to the edge of the shingle beach by one of the small paths. You can't follow the path across the field (it is being used as a caravan site at the time of writing) as

there's no right of way. Walk along the path on the narrow dyke at the edge of the beach, and follow it round to the right, up the river-bank. Stay on this path, over several gates, until you arrive at Exceat Bridge, which carries the main road over the river. Car owners should turn right, and walk along the side of the road, back to Westdean Corner and the car. If you've come by bus, you can wait for one at the Bridge, where there's a request stop.

Stage Three: Short-cut – Friston Corner to Seven Sisters – $1\frac{1}{2}$ miles. Walk down the road, by the side of the church, sign-posted 'Crowlink'. The road soon becomes a gravel track. Walk past the car-park and through the gate at the end. Bear left on to the grass track that goes through a gap in the gorse bushes. Just keep going over the Down, through a gate, to the cliff-edge. Here turn right, along the Seven Sisters, to pick up the main walk again.

---

4   *Eastdean – Birling Gap – Crowlink – Friston Corner –*
        Eastdean $4\frac{1}{2}$ miles

General Description This is a short circular using some of the paths described for the last walk. It's all on the Downs and makes a pleasant stroll of some $4\frac{1}{2}$ miles.

Maps As for the last walk.

To get to Eastdean Either take the Southdown bus 12 to the Eastdean stop and walk down into the village along the signposted lane, or the service 197 from Eastbourne and get off in the village. By car, drive along the A259 and turn off down to the village green where you can park.

To do the Walk Follow Stage Two of the instructions for Walk 3 as far as the Seven Sisters. On top of the second hill along towards Cuckmere Haven from Birling Gap there's a monument where you should turn right. Follow the grass track over the Down, through a gate, and along the hill, passing the roofs of Crowlink in the valley below to your left. Go through a gap in the gorse bushes and along the chalk track past the car-park on your left to the main road by the church. Turn right and walk down the narrow tarmac path indicated by the green metal post by the bus shelter. This path brings you out in Eastdean village again close to the Tiger Inn.

5 *Lewes – Mount Harry – Blackcap – Newmarket Inn –*
Newmarket Hill – Jugg's Road – Kingston – Lewes 12 miles

General Description I didn't think the book would be complete
without a circular based on Lewes. In order to ring the changes
we looked into the possibilities of walking over Mount Caburn,
Cliffe Hill, and Malling Hill, but unfortunately there weren't
enough public rights of way to make a suitable round trip.
Nevertheless I hope you'll appreciate the one I have chosen even
though it uses a short section of Walk 8.
After a climb from the prison you will pass the old racecourse.
Racing started here in the early eighteenth century – the grand-
stand was built in 1772. Up on the right from here is Mount Harry
where Simon de Montfort's men clambered up to fight the Battle
of Lewes in 1264, defeating the King, Henry III; this encounter
led to the first parliament of 1265. Past Mount Harry is Blackcap,
which is worth walking up to see the superb view of the Sussex
and Kent Wealds. Turning sharp left down the South Downs
Way you cross the A27 by the Newmarket Inn which makes a
convenient stop.
From here the walk goes up Newmarket Hill – where the right of
way has been diverted to our advantage – along the Jugg's Road,
and so down into Kingston. From here you go along the ridge
until you turn off across some fields to come out where you started.

How to get to Lewes By bus: there are a number of Southdown
services which you can catch. You should get off at the Prison Cross
Roads and walk a few yards up the Chailey Road. By car you should
make for the same spot – you can park your car in one of the side
roads near the prison.

Maps The two-and-a-half-inch Ordnance Survey Maps would be
best, but four of them are needed: TQ 20/30 (Brighton), TQ 21/31
(Burgess Hill), TQ 41 (Lewes) and TQ 40 (Newhaven), although
all but the extreme start and finish is on the first two of them. The
one-inch Sheet is 183 (Eastbourne). Our map is on page 26.

Stage One: Lewes Prison to Newmarket Inn – 6½ miles Take
the private road a few yards up the Chailey Road on the left. You
will pass some stables on your left. Bear round to the left by the
wall. Ahead you will see some footpaths signposted – take the right
fork here. This path, rather rutted in places, will take you round

and up the hill to the racecourse. Keep on past some gallops on the right (you should note they aren't a right of way), and past the stands on the left. You will eventually come to a firm track which goes up the hill. At the end of the racecourse keep straight on through a gate and past Mount Harry and Blackcap. On the way you'll see a rectangular clump of trees in the distance just to the left of the track. When you reach it go through a gate and turn left along the fence. There is a stone sign half-buried in the grass at the gate that tells you you're on the South Downs Way.

Continue along this track through a series of closely-spaced gates. Just past them turn left along another track where a sign indicates the South Downs Way. Go down the long hill, into a wood at the bottom. Walk through the wood on to a path at the other side which brings you out through a gate on to the A27, by the New-market Inn and the petrol station.

Stage Two: Newmarket Inn to Lewes – 5½ miles By the petrol station, take the concrete path under the railway arch, on to a green track that leads you up the hill passing the Newmarket Plantation on the right. The track now swings round to the left and joins the Jugg's Road by a five-barred gate. Go through this and up the hill by the new fence, down the other side, through a gate and bear left on to a chalk track.

This becomes very steep in places, leading you down to a metalled road past some houses. Go over the lane and past a few more houses. Jugg's Road now becomes a farm track across the middle of a field. After you have passed some allotments on your left look for the path, also on your left, which leads to two gates into a field by a bungalow. Walk diagonally down across this field to an iron gate. On the other side cross a smaller field then go through a gate and under the railway arch to the main road. Cross this and go up the bridle path the other side. At the first opportunity clamber up the path on the right and join another, going along by some gardens. This brings you out where you started, by the prison wall.

 6 *Woodingdean – Balsdean – Highdole Hill – Rodmell – Jugg's Road – Woodingdean* 6, 10 or 12 miles

General Description Only a few minutes' walk will take you away from civilisation altogether into bleak open downland.

Lying in a valley is the deserted hamlet of Balsdean: there was once an ancient chapel here but it was destroyed in the war. All that can be seen now is a cow byre and the floor of the farmhouse – but the spirits seem to linger here. I've described a short version of this walk that takes you up Balsdean Bottom to Kingston Hill but the main walk takes you over the ridge and down into Breaky Bottom – the farm there seems to have a faintly sinister air, and reminds me of the hideout, Breaky Hollow, in the Australian classic *Robbery Under Arms* by Rolf Boldrewood. Soon you arrive on the ridge of the Downs overlooking the Ouse valley and the hills beyond. There's another diversion here to allow you to descend to Rodmell to refresh yourself at the inn there.

The main walk continues along the ridge to Kingston Hill where you come across an ancient trackway – Jugg's Road – that drops steeply down into Kingston. Along this road the fishermen of Brighton used to bring their fish for sale in Lewes; it was at one time much used by smugglers too. On the way back to Woodingdean along this road you'll have some splendid views over the valley to Plumpton Plain where there are some other excellent walks that I've described elsewhere in this book.

To get to Woodingdean catch one of the local buses, 2, 6, 45 or 48, to the Downs Hotel. Walk up the Falmer Road past the bakery on the right. If you're coming by car turn into the Falmer Road at the Downs Hotel and park in McWilliam Road – a turning to the left about 110 yards up.

Maps Most of the walk is on TQ 20/30 (Brighton), but you will need TQ 40 (Newhaven) at one point. The one-inch Map is more convenient – you will need Sheet 183 (Eastbourne). See our map on page 26.

Stage One: Woodingdean to Mill Hill – 5 miles Walk up the Falmer Road on the right-hand side. Twenty-five yards past Bexhill Road you'll see a track on the right that immediately forks – it's marked by two green finger posts. Take the right fork. After a quarter of a mile take the left fork. Walk down the track for another quarter mile keeping the fence close on your right. On a fine day there are magnificent views to the left down into Newmarket Bottom and across to the Downs on the other side. Go through a stile and continue along the track, which is now unfenced, for about a mile and a half. It curves round to the right for most of that time but shortly after passing the remains of Balsdean in the valley below it curves round quite steeply and takes you down into the Bottom.

After a little way the track curves sharply left taking you along the other side of the valley. Go through two gates and alongside the row of beech trees into the cutting. You come out of it at a meeting of the ways not 200 yards from Balsdean. Here, you have to decide whether you want the long or short walk.

For the shorter one turn left, along a track that takes you past the barn. Bear right here and stay on the track: it leads you through the valley bottom (Balsdean Bottom) and eventually brings you out at a gate at the crest of the Downs above Kingston. Go through the gate and turn left. You are now back on the main walk, and can pick up the directions again.

For the long walk turn half-right along the dirt track leading round the side of the hill into the valley. Don't take the grass track that goes uphill in a cutting – that would take you back to Woodingdean. After a quarter of a mile take the left fork over the small hill. Just over the hill the track bears round to the right. About 25 yards before it runs into the metalled road to Balsdean Pumping Station turn hard left and follow a grass track down into the little valley and up the other side. Go through a gate near the top of the hill and keep to the right of the fence. Just at the crest of the hill turn right into the chalk track. Keep on this, passing just to the right of the grey barn. Go through the metal gate here, and keep over to the fence on the left. Once through the metal gate at the far side of this field you will be on a fenced track. Go down this for about $\frac{1}{4}$ mile. Turn left into a fenced, slightly overgrown, grass track (there is a stone footpath sign at the entrance with its back to you pointing out the way). This path turns right after a little way and then left 100 yards further on. Go through the gate here and walk down the right-hand side of the fence into Breaky Bottom; you arrive not far from those sinister-looking farm buildings I was telling you about. Turn left through a gateway and immediately right up the hill along a track. Go through the gate at the top of the hill and past the barn in the next dip to another gate at the top of the next rise, on the other side of which a concrete road leads steeply down into the river valley. Don't go through the gate, but through one of the wire gates just on this side. Go left if you want to continue the walk without a break and right if you want to go down into Rodmell, to refresh yourself at the Abergavenny Arms. This involves a further 2 miles walking.

To get to Rodmell turn right, and walk along the side of the field with the fence on your left, to the gate at the top of the next rise by the bushes. On the other side there's a narrow path that

takes you out on to a metalled road. Turn left down the hill into
Rodmell. The inn is opposite you on the main road. To continue
the walk retrace your steps to the gates by the concrete road.

Stage Two: Mill Hill to Woodingdean – 5 miles Turn left,
through the other wire gate along the right-hand side of the field.
At the far end, there's a gate giving access to a T-junction of
concrete roads which, I should warn you, are sometimes used for
motor-cycle scrambles. Walk up the one in front of you for about
$1\frac{1}{4}$ miles until it turns sharply left. Here leave it by turning right,
along the fence for 100 yards and through the gate in the
corner. Turn left along the fence. The path quickly becomes a
track which you follow for about a mile. The track turns left
through a gate and down into Balsdean Bottom. If you've taken the
short walk you will come out here. Stay on the uphill side of the
fence and go through a gate a hundred yards in front of you. Follow
the grass track. After some while bear left through a gateway past
some gorse bushes and bear slightly left up the hill along the grass
track to the fence. Follow the fence to the gate. Go along the chalk
track for about $1\frac{1}{2}$ miles past a radio mast and so back into
Woodingdean.

---

7 *Roedean – Ovingdean – Mount Pleasant – Woodingdean –
Racecourse – Roedean* $4\frac{1}{2}$ miles

General Description This walk can be done in $1\frac{1}{2}$ to 2 hours.
Unfortunately you never lose sight of buildings although in
compensation you often have commanding views of the Downs
and sea. Ovingdean is a place that always delights with its squat
Saxon church and the remains of the Grange – the subject of a
novel by Harrison Ainsworth. You then walk over Mount Pleasant to
Woodingdean, return to Roedean by the racecourse and the
golf course, and have some impressive views of the sea and Roedean
School.

To get to Roedean take the 7, 47, 12, 12a, 12b, 12c, 17, 39 or
55 bus to Roedean School. If you're travelling by car you will find
ample parking facilities on the corner of Roedean Road and the
Coast Road by the Miniature Golf Course on the Brighton side of
Roedean School.

Maps Either use the two-and-a-half-inch Ordnance Map, Sheet

TQ 20/30, or see our map on page 26. The one-inch Sheet doesn't show enough detail to follow this walk, and even the two-and-a-half-inch map hasn't all the paths marked.

The Walk From the car park go inland, over the mounds, to the corner of Roedean Way near the School. On the corner you will find a signposted path that takes you round the edge of a field. A little way past the second signpost turn right, through a wooden swing gate, up the hill – it is signposted to Ovingdean. Follow the path up the hill, through a second gate, along the side of the field, through a third gate, and down the other side of the hill. Go through the fourth gate in the wall by the churchyard, down the steps, and across the field below to the gate in the middle of the far wall.

Cross the road and walk up the lane opposite. At the crest of the hill you will see a footpath sign on the left pointing to a good chalk track that will take you over Mount Pleasant to Woodingdean with Happy Valley on your right. Walk up the road by the school and cross Warren Road. You can break for refreshment at the Downs Hotel a few yards to your right. Walk up Downsway to the top. Turn right, and almost immediately left on to the Falmer Road. About 100 yards up on the left there is a bridleway sign indicating a track. This track takes you along the back of the houses and bungalows on a ridge of the Downs. At the end of the houses take the path to the left, passing the railed-in waterworks site on your right. Go across the green by the bus stop and over the road to the corner of the racecourse.

Follow this path straight down for 1 mile, keeping both the race-course and the golf course on your right. At a T-junction turn right, and immediately bear left up the hill. Follow the track round to the left, but don't go through the gate: instead, keep to the right of the fence, and walk down the side of the field towards the school. This path will bring you back to where you started.

---

8 *Falmer – St Mary's Farm – Streathill Farm – Buckland Bank – Waterpit Hill – Falmer* 4½ miles

---

General Description Falmer, despite its ultra-modern twentieth-century surroundings, has remained firmly in the nineteenth. In this respect it is like Stanmer, just up the road. This walk, although a short one, contains a great deal of historical interest. You stride along to St Mary's Farm, pleasantly situated in a hollow, and on to Streathill Farm, a landmark you can pick out from miles away. Thence a short piece along the South Downs Way. The view over Streat, Plumpton, and East Chiltington seems wilder than most views over the Weald. On your right you'll be able to pick out a large Bronze Age Settlement and ahead the lonely Blackcap. When you turn right towards home there is Buckland Bank on your left where there are remains of a Roman 'circus', or meeting place. Further on is Balmer, now only a farm, but once a mediaeval village the last traces of which were destroyed when the area was used as an artillery range in the war. Just hereabouts you will catch a surprising view of Mt Caburn, Firle Beacon, and Seaford Head all at once, when you're least expecting it. When you return to Falmer, if you have time, you may like to cross the main road to visit the pond and view the other side of the Downs.

How to Get There If you are travelling by car drive out on the Lewes Road to Falmer. Turn left up Ridge Road, past the University Sports Field, to the very top of the lane where there is a gate across the way and a sign saying 'No Through Road – St Mary's Farm Only'. Park near here. By bus, you should catch one of the many Southdown services plying between Brighton and Lewes and get off at The Swan at Falmer. Walk up the hill, along Ridge Road, to the entrance to St Mary's Farm. If you come by bus the walk will be 1½ miles longer.

Maps It is better to use the two-and-a-half-inch Ordnance Survey Maps: Sheets TQ 20/30 (Brighton) and TQ 21/31 (Burgess Hill). The one-inch maps are very inconvenient as the walk is on the border between Sheets 182 and 183. See our map on page 26.

The Walk However you have arrived at the entrance to St Mary's Farm, walk through the gate and along the metalled lane down into the valley. Go through the white gate and past the farm buildings to the end of the concrete road. Turn right by the cottages through a gate and up the hill. Twenty-five yards up bear left, so as to go down the left-hand side of a copse. Follow this track through various gates for one mile. You will pass Streathill Farm on your left, clearly distinguishable by the large silo. A quarter mile further on go through a gate and turn right on to a chalk track – the South Downs Way. After a further quarter mile you will meet the end of a tarmac road coming up from Plumpton. Bear half-right here, to continue along the track round the side of a field or two, until you

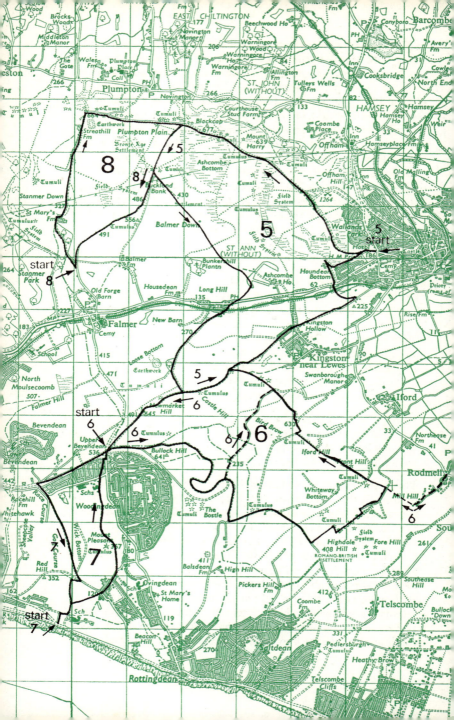

come to a plantation of trees at a little distance to the right. Walk past it to a gate in the track at the far end. Don't go through the gate but turn right, along the fence. There is a marker by the gate that shows you are following the South Downs Way by doing so. Walk down by the edge of the trees. Go through a gate and along the left-hand side of a field through a series of closely spaced gates. Keep going straight ahead – don't turn left here to follow the South Downs Way. Three hundred yards further on take the right fork in the track round the side of the hill (Balmer Huff). Just keep going – the track eventually runs out into the metalled lane that brought you up from Falmer village. The entrance to St Mary's Farm is on the right, about 100 yards up the hill. Either collect your car or walk back down into Falmer.

---

9   *Patcham – The Chattri – Ditchling Beacon – Stanmer Park*
7 miles

General Description I do hope you'll forgive me for not making this one a circular, but it doesn't really lend itself, since the path you need to use, to make it one, entails a rather dreary and disappointing finish. For all that, this book wouldn't be complete without it. You have excellent public transport facilities, and can't lose by not being able to take advantage of return bus fares, as the local bus operators don't issue them. Patcham Village itself still retains its dignity, with All Saints Church – which contains one of the few 'Doom' paintings – together with some very pleasant old cottages, and the ancient dovecote, not forgetting the fountain. You will go over the fields to the Chattri, which must be unique in this country: an Indian shrine set alone on the Downs, watching over their dead of that terrible First World War. Fairly soon you'll join our old friend, the South Downs Way, which takes you to Ditchling Beacon – one of the highest points on the Downs – now sadly affected by the presence of the car park, useful though it may be.

From here inland again, through the majestic woods of Stanmer Park, to the village itself. There you will find a useful shop with a café. From there, you walk on through the park, past the attractive Georgian Mansion, once the home of the Pelham family, to the main Brighton–Lewes Road.

To Get to Patcham either take a Brighton, Hove and District Red bus (Numbers 5 or 5b) to the Ladies Mile Hotel and walk up Vale Avenue, or catch one of the many Southdown buses that go up the London Road. Get off at The Black Lion and go up the lane by the side of the pub which will bring you out in Vale Avenue at the starting point of the walk. By car: drive up Vale Avenue and park somewhere near the turning at the top of the hill.

Maps By far the best maps are the two-and-a-half-inch Sheets TQ 20/30 (Brighton) and TQ 21/31 (Burgess Hill). You can use the one-inch Sheet 182 (Brighton and Worthing) but the detail is inadequate in places. See our map on page 30.

Stage One: Patcham to Ditchling Beacon – $3\frac{1}{2}$ miles Opposite the top end of the lane coming up from the fountain past the church there is a metalled road leading past Patcham Court Farm and out on to the Downs. Walk up this for 200 or 300 yards. On the left there is a small gate with a notice by it referring to the Chattri. Walk across the field, bearing slightly left – there isn't much sign of a path to start with. At the far end go through a gate. On the other side you'll find a well-defined path that takes you up to a clump of trees which you can see in the distance with the white dome of the Chattri beside it. As you come closer, you'll find that the Chattri is off the path some yards to the right. Continue along the path, bearing right by the small clump of trees, and over several fields to the crest of the Downs.

Here turn sharp right through a gate and follow the South Downs Way along the edge of the scarp slope of the Downs. After going a mile and a quarter and through three gates you will come to Ditchling Beacon.

Stage Two: Ditchling Beacon to Stanmer Park – $3\frac{1}{2}$ miles Cross the road here and go through the gate on the other side leading back on to the Downs. About a quarter of a mile further on you will find a gate on the right by some gorse bushes giving access to a path leading at about '2 o'clock' across a field, which is cultivated but with the path left clear. Go into a second field and down a hill into a dip and up the other side. Here turn right, through a gate and down into a hollow. Keeping to the right-hand side of this hollow you will shortly see a notice pointing out a right of way to the right through a gate into Stanmer Woods. Walk up the hill, over a cross-paths, and down the other side. Leave the belt of trees on your right and continue down the path into the village. Walk through the village and bear left at the fork. This road will bring you out after $\frac{3}{4}$ mile, at the main gates of Stanmer Park.

To get home you can catch one of the many Southdown buses which pass the entrance – to the left for Lewes, to the right for Brighton.

IO   *Hurstpierpoint – Danny Park – Wolstonbury – Pyecombe – Sweet Hill – Patcham*   7 miles

---

General Description We start this time at Hurstpierpoint, a small town in the Weald. The church was almost completely rebuilt in the last century by Sir Charles Barry, the architect of the Houses of Parliament. It's notable for its spire, which can be seen for miles around. The paths you take are rather fun – going in and out of fields and woods across to Danny Park. The house is an impressive example of the Elizabethan 'E' shape, having been built in 1582 by the Goring Family. The British Cabinet met there in 1918 to decide on peace terms with Germany. The steep climb up Wolstonbury I'm sure you'll find worthwhile. This odd whalelike hill sticks out majestically into the Weald. At its crest, there are the remains of an Iron Age earthwork. You descend from here to Pyecombe which nestles in a fold of the Downs and was once the centre of the crook-making industry. The church here has one of the three lead fonts in Sussex. Here you can call it a day, and catch the bus home, or cross the road and walk up on to the Downs past the riding stables. Here a nice clear path will take you along the ridge over Sweet Hill to Patcham, on the outskirts of Brighton.

How to get to Hurstpierpoint Take a Southdown bus, Service 14, 23 or 24, from Pool Valley or wherever convenient to Hurstpierpoint church. This walk is not designed for car owners but if you want to try it and catch the bus back from Patcham to collect your car there is a car park in South Avenue in Hurstpierpoint.

Maps If you want to take a map you should use the two-and-a-half-inch Ordnance Survey Maps, Sheets TQ 21/31 (Burgess Hill) and TQ 20/30 (Brighton). The one-inch Sheet 182 gives a general idea of the countryside, but not sufficient detail to follow the walk. See our map on page 30.

Stage One: Hurstpierpoint to Pyecombe – 4½ miles Which side of the road you get out on depends on which bus you've caught. Either way walk eastwards from the church along the High Street towards Hassocks. Turn right down South Avenue. You will see a

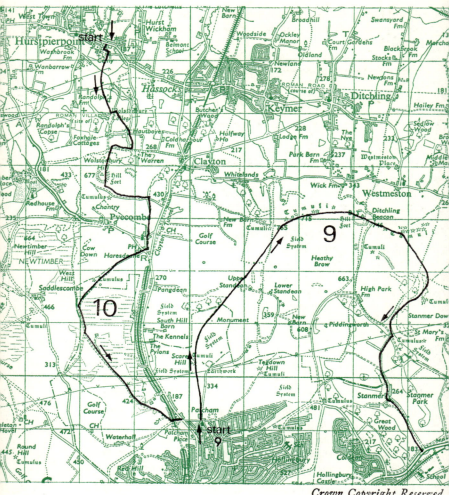

row of houses on your left and recreation ground on the right.
Just past the end of the open space you'll find a cinder track turning
off to the left between the houses with a 'cycling prohibited' sign at
the entrance.

Walk down past some gardens, until you come to a field on the
right. Almost on the corner you'll find a squeeze gate that gives on
to a path through a field, skirting a hedge at the right. Go
through the gate on the far side and bear slightly right on to a

track across a second field. Cross a small stream by a plank bridge and so arrive at a third field. Stop following the track here – it goes off in the general direction of a house half-right – instead, turn to face the wood, and go into it through a small gate. This wood is only about 100 yards thick. Cross the field on the other side by the path that's been left at the left-hand side and go through a swing gate into yet another field, this time with oak trees in it. Leave this field by the bottom left corner, at the edge of a clump of trees, by going through a squeeze gate, over a plank bridge, and through a second squeeze gate. A little way on go through a third such gate, and so out on to the drive by Danny House. Turn left and walk down the drive for 100 yards until you come to a footpath sign. Go into the field and follow the track through the metal gate and diagonally across the second field, as though towards the Downs, aiming for a point about 50 yards in from the left-hand edge of the small wood you'll see ahead of you. About two-thirds of the way across you will have to go through a gate left in a wire fence.

Go through the narrow wood and out on to New Way Lane. Turn right and follow it for about 300 yards until the lane turns sharp left. Leave it here by turning right, through a gate with a notice on it, saying 'Danny Estate – please keep your dogs on leads'. Walk along the track parallel to the Downs and turn left at the T-junction. Just inside the trees at the base of the hill you'll find the remains of a stile, it is quite easy to get over. Bear slightly right up the slope for a few yards and then take the steepest path (and it's *very* steep) up the hill. At the top of this hill – Wolstonbury Hill – there's an Ordnance Survey triangulation pillar. Stop here for a while – there are some quite magnificent views. You're nearly 700 feet above sea level, and looking out over the Weald on a fine day you can see the North Downs.

Go straight across the hill. You will come to a stile: go over this and across the field by the path that's been left. Turn left on to the main track, as though heading towards the twin windmills Jack and Jill across the valley. Go down the hill for some way until you come to a metal gate across the track. Go through this and turn right, about 25 yards further on, into a well-cared-for track between hedges. This will bring you out into Pyecombe Village. Walk down to the main road, passing the Church on the way. At the main road there's a pub – The Plough – which serves snacks and is a good place to break your walk. If you feel you've had enough, this is the place to stop – buses going into Brighton pass here at frequent intervals.

Stage Two: Pyecombe to Patcham – 2½ miles Cross the road from The Plough – be careful, there's fast traffic here – and walk up the track by the sign 'Brendon Riding School'. Go through a gate, up the hill to the top, through another gate and (bearing left) on to a main track. Follow this for about 1½ miles: you will come out at the top of a hill overlooking the Waterhall Pumping Station. Go down the hill and under the railway bridge; this brings you out on the main London Road at the traffic lights by the garage.

To get home walk down to The Black Lion where there is a choice of buses to take you back into Brighton. If you want to get back to Hurstpierpoint the 14 and 24 pass here – there's a stop by the garage.

II *Hangleton – Devil's Dyke – Fulking Hill – Foredown Hospital – Hangleton*   7½ miles

---

General Description Most local people know the 'walk to the Dyke'; if they haven't done it themselves they will know someone who has. There are various ways of going there, but this is the best if you want to avoid the roads. Hangleton is an easy place to reach by car or bus. The Church and Manor stood for centuries in lonely state – even as recently as 1931 the population was only 109. Now it is bursting at the seams and the houses have covered over the remains of the mediaeval village. You wander first across the West Hove golf course, then across the Downs, noticing, on the right, Hangleton Round Hill. The Devil's Dyke itself is a popular spot for people coming to see the panoramic view across the Weald. Just below you can see the pleasant villages of Poynings and Fulking. Close to the Devil's Dyke Hotel there is the Dyke itself, with the graves of the Devil and his wife in the bottom. This deep, steep-sided valley was supposed in local legend to have been dug by the Devil in the space of a night to let the sea in and drown the churches in the Weald. But he could only work at night so an old woman foiled him by putting a candle in a sieve to represent the rising sun, forcing him to leave off his work. The rest of the walk is on pleasant downland over Fulking Hill and Mount Zion to Portslade, and so back to Hangleton.

To get to the starting point take the local red bus: either Service 8 to the corner of Hangleton Valley Drive and Hangleton Lane or Service 5b to Towns Corner and walk down Hangleton

Lane to the corner of Hangleton Valley Drive. By car: drive to this corner and park in one of the side roads.

Maps The best maps here are our old favourites TQ 20/30 (Brighton) and TQ 21/31 (Burgess Hill). See our map on page 34.

Stage One: Hangleton to The Devil's Dyke – 3½ miles From the corner of Hangleton Valley Drive and Hangleton Lane walk up the lane for 25 yards. Turn right into an unmade road marked as a public footpath. Go down to the cottages at the end, turn left and then right – up the side of the golf course – keeping to the left of the hedge. At the end of the hedge the track also ends, leaving only a faintly-marked grass path. Follow this straight ahead up the hill aiming to pass just to the right of the clump of bushes. Pass between the bushes and a green on your right and continue up the path over the top of the hill. Ahead of you another clump of bushes should shortly appear. Walk up to them, keeping the next green on your left. There is a narrow path, through these bushes and the rough ground to the side of them; this takes you to a barrier of poles across the path which you'll have to climb over. On the other side is a track which you should follow for 2 miles across the Downs. It goes through two gates and brings you out on the road by the Dyke. Turn left and walk up it, passing the Dyke itself on the right, to the Hotel.

Stage Two: The Dyke to Hangleton – 4 miles At the Hotel turn left off the road at the point where it turns to the right, round the end of the building, and becomes an open space. Cross the rough grass to the stile. After climbing over it walk straight ahead along the path, past the ruined building just to your left, and through the patch of rough ground. Walk along the sward bearing half-left to make for a gate across a main track. Once through this gate follow the track for 25 yards then turn left along an unfenced track across a field. Go over the brow. After half a mile, just before you come to the corner of the field, turn left through a gate and down a dead-straight track with a fence on the right. This leads you to the Foredown Isolation Hospital.

If you need to travel home by bus walk straight ahead of you to the Mill Inn where there is a stop for the Service 11. If you need to get back to your car in Hangleton take the first turning to the left past the Hospital down a poorly-asphalted unmarked lane that brings you out in Hangleton Lane. Walk down the road in front of you and bear a fraction left on to the narrow lane, between hedgerows, that takes you across the golf links. This brings you out once more at the corner of Hangleton Valley Drive.

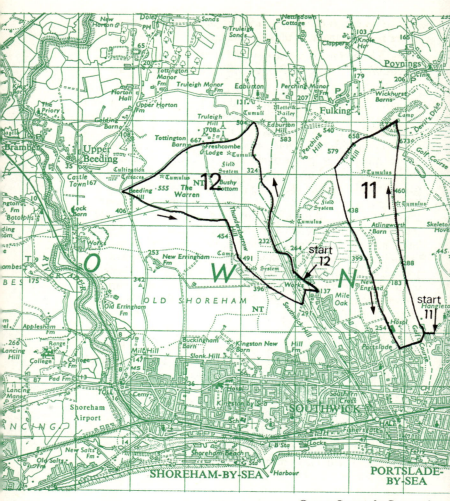

Crown Copyright Reserved

---

12   *Mile Oak – Edburton Hill – Truleigh Hill – Beeding Hill – Thundersbarrow Hill – Mile Oak*   **7 miles**

General Description   This walk begins at the far end of the new suburb of Mile Oak. As you come up the main road you can see a few traces of the much older buildings that have been overrun by the new housing. Many of the hills and valleys you'll pass on this walk have been given pleasant names that makes it fun to pick them out from a map. You'll pass Whitelot and Hazelholt Bottoms, with Cockroost Hill on your right. After passing through Summers Deane you come out on Edburton Hill with its magnificent views over the Weald. On the slope of this hill are the earthworks of a mediaeval castle. At the foot of the hill is Edburton Church which has one of the three leaden fonts in Sussex. You'll be walking along our old friend the South Downs Way for a while to Beeding Hill where you'll have a splendid view of Bramber, Beeding and Steyning, with entrancing tree-capped Chanctonbury in the distance. You return to Mile Oak by The Warren and Thundersbarrow Hill. The whole walk is on open downland. Regrettably there's no possible stop for refreshment.

How to get there By car: drive up the Mile Oak Road from Portslade to its end. There is room to park here, so long as you don't obstruct the farm entrance. By bus: catch Service 26, and get out at Chrisdory Road, or the 15 or 55 to the terminus, and go up Chalky Road to the Mile Oak Road. In either case, walk up to the end of Mile Oak Road.

Maps Either the one-inch Ordnance Survey Map, Sheet 182 (Brighton and Worthing), or the two two-and-a-half-inch Sheets TQ 20/30 (Brighton) and TQ 21/31 (Burgess Hill). Our map is on page 34.

Stage One: Mile Oak to Beeding Hill – 3½ miles Continue along the line of the road through the gate and along the farm drive. Keep straight ahead along the valley bottom and round the side of the hill. After 1¼ miles you will come to the second of two cattle grids. Just on the other side take the left fork. This green track will take you through a gate by some woods on to another track which eventually leads out on to the South Downs Way at the edge of the Downs. Turn left, up Truleigh Hill, and keep on the track which shortly becomes a metalled road and leads you past some houses to the top of Beeding Hill. Here there is a meeting of six ways, and the road turns sharp left.

Stage Two: Beeding Hill to Mile Oak – 3½ miles Leave the metalled road by turning even sharper left on to a path in the angle of the road. Keep on this path for a good mile down into the valley and up the other side. Turn right at the T-junction. This track takes you across Thundersbarrow Hill into some heath-like country. Here the track is used by horses, and it often becomes rather muddy and sticky. To avoid it climb over the stile at your left, into the National Trust property. Soon turn right, through gorse bushes, into a narrow path. If you follow this, ignoring the other paths you cross, it will eventually take you into a field. Here there's another stile, which you can cross to regain the original path. Very soon you should turn left through a gate into a large field. Now take the path on your left, going steeply down the hill, through two gates. By the second gate take the path on the right, which crosses a field by the backs of the houses. This will lead you back on to the Mile Oak Road.

---

13   *North Lancing – Steep Down – Cissbury Ring – Chanctonbury Ring – Coombes – North Lancing*   11 to 14 miles

---

General Description Whenever anyone from the big city suggests coming down at the weekend to go for a walk I recommend this one. It is very straightforward, unless you do the excursion towards Coombes, and it's immensely satisfying. There is good parking at Lancing Ring. You pass Steep Down (which seems a misnomer) on your way to Cissbury Ring. I worry a little that I'm including too much information about archaeological sites, but at Cissbury there is a very important Iron Age earthwork, and it is worthwhile walking round the ramparts, to see the partly-filled-in shafts of the much older Stone Age flint mines. If you're thirsty you can detour to Findon, but the walk continues along the Downs to Chanctonbury Hill, which is another Iron Age camp and the site of an ancient temple where witches are still said to gather at the main festivals of the year. The beech trees themselves have an interesting history: they were sown by a Mr Charles Goring of Wiston House in 1760, who luckily lived long enough to see them grow – it's reputed he carried buckets of water up the hill every day in summer to ensure they didn't die of drought.

Carrying on from Chanctonbury you catch a glimpse of Bramber and Steyning and can look out over the Adur Valley. I have included the section to Coombes to allow you to pop down to see the fascinating little twelfth-century church there, which has some rare wall paintings, dating from the late 1100s, only recently uncovered during restoration.

To get to North Lancing by bus: catch Southdown
Service 9 from Brighton, or the 207/217 from Worthing,
and get off at the roundabout at North Lancing – the stop is
called 'Lancing Manor'. By car: drive out on the A27 to the same
roundabout and turn off up the road marked 'North Lancing'.
After a few yards the road bears round to the left, here turn right
up Mill Road. Drive to the top and park on the grass at the very
end of the tarmac road.

Maps The most useful map for this walk is the Ordnance Survey
one-inch Sheet 182 (Brighton and Worthing). The two-and-a-half-
inch Sheets are TQ 10 and TQ 11. See our map on page 39.

Stage One: North Lancing to Cissbury Ring – 3½ miles Walk
up the continuation of Mill Road, past the riding stables on to the
Downland track. After a few yards you'll pass the trees of Lancing
Ring on the left. Keep ahead, along the track, passing between the
trees and the fence on the right. The track unwinds ahead of you for
1½ miles, taking you round the side of Steep Down, and brings you
out at a large cross-paths by an electricity pylon. Here turn left,
on to another track, which takes you down into a hollow and up the
other side to the road.

Cross the road and go down the track on the other side. After a
quarter of a mile you will come to a meeting of several tracks. Take
either of the ones more or less in front of you, which join up after
a little way, and take you down the hill and up the other side to
Cissbury. On the way you will pass a white barn close under
Cissbury Hill. Keep straight ahead up to the crest of the hill where
you will find a car park and the top end of the metalled road
coming up from Findon. If you want some refreshment walk
down this road for about a mile, into Findon Village, and to the
Gun Inn. Afterwards retrace your steps to the car park by Cissbury
Ring.

Stage Two: Cissbury Ring to Steep Down – 5 miles From
Cissbury turn through the car park and go along the track at the
end. Keep on this track for two miles. Don't turn off along any
marked ways. Just after a sign in the hedge 'to Steyning' take the
right fork and half a mile further on again take the right fork. The
track you're on is not signposted because strictly it isn't a footpath
or bridleway for much of its length – it's an ancient highway, which
can be used by vehicles – thus explaining the highway style of sign
at one point. After the two miles, you will go over the crest of a
small hill and down to a junction of paths. Your path turns to the
left and becomes a grass track leading up to a gate. Go this way if

you want to look at the trees on Chanctonbury Ring; otherwise turn right, through a gateway signposted 'South Downs Way'. Follow this track for 1½ miles until you come to what seems a T-junction of paths. Go straight across this other track and along a narrow path left in the middle of a field to the road beyond. (At the time of writing this, it's signposted 'South Downs Way Diversion'). Turn slightly right on to the road, and walk down it for about ¼ mile, until it bends away to the right. Here turn off half-left along a wide track, go over the top of the hill and down to the important cross-paths by the pylon you've passed once already. Here you have a choice – either walk back the way you started out, to Lancing, or turn off to Coombes, which will add a hilly extra 1½ miles to your walk.

Stage Three: Steep Down to Coombes and North Lancing – 3 miles At the cross-paths turn off through a gate into the field with the pylon in it. Go half-right across this field, following the grass track, to meet up with the fence on the Lancing side – ignore the track that goes down into the valley bottom. Walk alongside the fence to the top of the next hill, to end up just to the right of the clump of trees at its crest.

Just by the trees there is a gateway with two tracks leading away on the other side. Don't go through the gateway but turn right along the fence keeping it to your left. Keep going along here – there's no very clear path – until you reach a clump of trees by a gate. Walk alongside the trees for 25 yards and then turn left down the slope and through a small gate into the trees. Walk down the path to the church. To return, retrace your steps to the gate at the top of the hill. Here strike out, with your back to the trees, up the slope and over the crest of the hill. You will come to the corner of a fence. Bear slightly left and walk down the side of the fence to a gate and stile at the end of the field. Go over the stile and along the track, with the fence at your left. Where the track bears left keep straight on along the edge of the field with the line of trees on your left. Go over the remains of a stile at the corner of the field, across the track, and down the other side – again to the right of the trees, to the barn in the bottom (called Cowbottom Hovel). Once past the hovel walk up the hill, to the stile at the very top, keeping the fence to your right. Once over the stile you have a problem; at the time of writing the farmer hasn't left a path through his field, and you can't see the stile on the other side to aim for. I suggest that, if there's still no path visible, you turn left and walk round three sides of this field ignoring the stile in the left-hand fence and the gate in the corner. If you walk along the side of the field

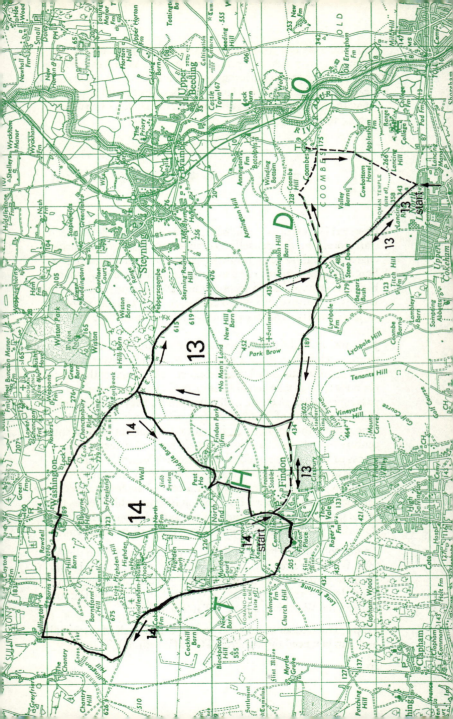

opposite to the one you entered by you will come to another stile on the left. Go over this, straight down the slope, and up the other side to yet another stile. This brings you out into the open space used as a car park at the top of Mill Road. Either collect your car or turn left along the main track a few yards in from the fence and go down into Lancing.

14 *Findon – Sullington – Washington – Chanctonbury Ring – Findon* 9 miles

General Description Findon makes a very agreeable centre to start from. The village itself has retained much of its old-world charm, thankfully being firmly by-passed by the main road. Every September 24th there is a mammoth sheep fair here which dates back for centuries. Then sheep would have been driven across the Downs, over the paths we walk now, instead of arriving in lorries as they do today. There is a famous cricket ground close to the church.

Just away from the village in a magnificent setting of trees lie the church and Findon Place. From here to Sullington, you cross lovely open countryside by well-defined paths, leaving the site of the once famous mansion of Muntham Court on your right, and passing Highden Beeches. Sullington is still, happily, an unspoilt hamlet consisting of the Manor, farm, and church. If you have time it is worth popping into this church to look at the thirteenth-century monument of a knight in chain mail. The next stretch, across to Washington under the Downs, is pleasant. Washington itself is another by-passed village, dominated by Chanctonbury, which you climb up to in a low gear. From Chanctonbury back to Findon, you pass through Buddington Bottom, which seems to be full of game, and go past a turkey farm and a famous training stables. Although only nine miles long, this walk seems strenuous.

To get to Findon by car is simple – merely drive out on the A24 from Worthing and park somewhere in the village – there is parking about 50 yards from The Gun. By bus: you can catch any of the Southdown Service 201, 202, 205 or 211 that ply up the Findon Valley from Worthing, and get off at The Gun.

Maps The Ordnance Survey two-and-a-half-inch Maps would be best, but you need three sheets: TQ 10 (Worthing), TQ 11

(Steyning) and, for a short time only, TQ 01 (Storrington). The one-inch Sheet is Number 182 (Brighton and Worthing). See also our map on page 39.

Stage One: Findon to Washington – 4½ miles Walk due South down from the Gun Inn in Findon Village. Take the footpath by the Findon Village Hall, which goes across the middle of a field to a swing gate at the other end. Cross the A24 into the drive opposite and walk past Findon Place and the church. Go through a swing gate on to the path which dorders the wood and through another swing gate into a field. Here keep on the track straight in front of you up the hill, with the cricket ground on your right. Go over another stile into a field. Take the path across this to the gate. Cross the road and walk into the opening opposite. Here turn sharp right up a farm track. For a good mile and a half follow this track through fields and gates, passing some woods on the right and a farm at a distance on the left. Ignore all right and left turns and the track brings you to Highden Beeches. Here leave the chalk path and turn left by the dew pond. Keep on this path to the green corrugated iron barn on the South Downs Way. Here turn sharp right, and immediately left, on to a trackway going downhill. Bear left at the barn – this track takes you straight into Sullington. Just before the church turn right by a signpost into a field. Keep the hedge on the left-hand side all the way round the field to the gate at the far end by two tall trees. Go over another field to a gate by Barns Farm. Take the path in front of the house and brick potting shed through two gates. Then walk down the farm track, which continues past a house ½ mile ahead on the right, and so on to a metalled road with Rowdell House on the left. This takes you on a bridge over the A24 into Washington village.

Stage Two: Washington to Findon – 4½ miles Walk through the village to the old main road, where you turn left. After twenty yards turn right by a wooden signpost into a field. Clamber up a slope and over two stiles in front of you. Climb over a fence into a field on the right. Here turn left and keep to the path by the hedge past Tilleys Farm. At the end of the farm the path goes diagonally across three fields and over three stiles to a wood under the Downs. Turn left and quickly right, through a gate, and climb up the steep hill. Although it is a stiff climb there are some rewarding views at the top. Go through a gate and make for Chanctonbury Ring. At the Ring bear slightly right down the hill through a gate. Keep on for a quarter mile until you come to a cross-tracks. Turn right here and shortly right again through a gate on to another track. Go through a further gate. This takes you down into Buddington Bottom. Go through a gate into a wood, and then through another gate into a field. Here you should take the right fork. This path twists round a cultivated field until it brings you eventually into a wood. At the top of the slope cross over one path and turn right on to a metalled road. Walk down this, past the turkey houses on your right. By the signpost to a Pest House, go left through a gate into a field. Walk straight up the field to a gate. On the other side, go down the track opposite. This track takes you past Gallops Farm, into a dip. By a hedge on the right take the signposted bridlepath to a T-junction. Turn sharp left on to a road through the village to the Gun Inn.

---

15 *Patching Woods Circular* 7½ miles

General Description One point I should mention right at the start: you must follow the directions for this walk exactly, as otherwise you'll surely get lost – in a forest all the paths look alike and you can't see far enough to find out where you are.
Patching itself is a pleasant, quiet hamlet with a pretty row of houses and a church with a graceful spire. Most of the trees in the forest are deciduous and not so gloomy as the dark conifers. I'm purposely taking you to Barpham – now only a farm, but once a village with a church – which was pulled down in 1500. All that remains is the outline of the foundations on the grass. This must surely be one of the most remote and lonely stretches of the South Downs. You can see Harrow Hill on the right, an Iron Age fort, together with Black Patch. Both are famous for their Stone Age flint mines. In front of you, stretched out, are the Downs overlooking Storrington, and on the left, later on, you'll be able to see the Arun and Arundel Castle. The remainder of the walk needs little description except for some attractive cottages at one point and Dover House, nestling on the edge of the trees.

To get to the starting point by car turn off the A27, the Worthing to Arundel Road, at a signpost marked 'Patching Street Only'. Carry on until you can go no further. You can park on the road-edge. If you are using public transport you should catch the Southdown Service 9, get off at The Horse and Groom, turn into the lane, and walk up to the very end. This will add 1½ miles to the walk.

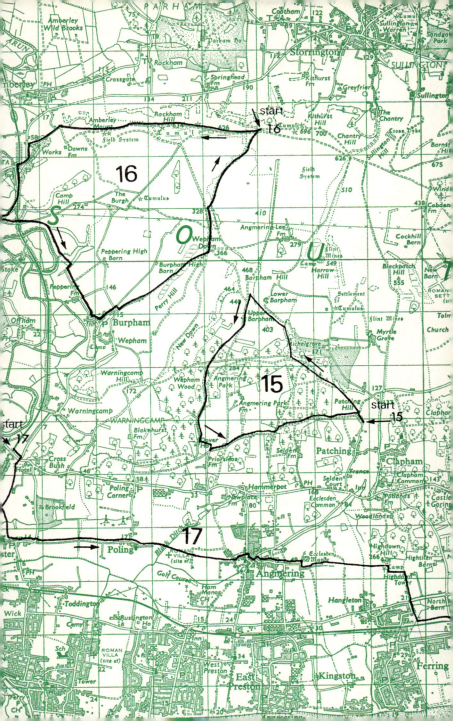

Maps I wouldn't rely on any Ordnance Survey Map, not even the two-and-a-half-inch ones, as many of the paths and rides in the forest aren't marked. Our general map of the area is on page 43.

The Walk Go through the gate at the end of the road and turn half-left along the bridleway. Keep firmly to the edge of the field which stretches for the best part of $\frac{3}{4}$ mile. At the end you will come to the wood, and should see a gate and a stile ahead of you leading into it. Go over the stile, bear round slightly to the left along the path, and after a few yards go over a second stile. Walk down the grass path in front of you, again bearing round to the left, but after a few yards turn slightly right, to walk straight down the wide ride between the trees. Go down this ride for about 250 yards until you come to a meeting of six ways marked by a signpost. Take the third one round, at about one o'clock, which is a narrow path marked by a 'footpath' sign.

Stay on this narrow path for about half a mile. You will cross one ride, at right angles to your direction of travel. At the second junction go straight ahead, down the wider ride signposted 'Bridleway'. Shortly you will come to a gate, at a slight angle on the left. Go through this and immediately turn right, along a path through the trees a little way to the left of the fence. After a $\frac{1}{4}$ mile you will come to a five-barred gate across the way. Go through this and take the right-hand path close to the fence on the right. After another 200 yards or so veer right, through another gate, and walk down the track parallel to the fence and a few feet to the right of it. Stay on this track, which runs along the top of a steep slope down to the right with Lower Barpham Farm in the valley below, for half a mile. Ignore the turnings-off down into the valley. At the end of this track turn left through a gate. Follow the hedge round to the left for a hundred yards or so. You will meet up with a main track coming in from the right. Follow this down through the gate, and past Upper Barpham Farm. A hundred yards past the farm turn right, through a gate, and immediately turn back left, to follow the edge of the field down for several hundred yards to the small gate in the bottom corner by the trees. Go through this gate, turn slightly left through the second gate, and then right, down the ride. At the big junction turn right, and then immediately half-left into the track going still in the same direction. You will pass some attractive cottages on the left. After about one mile, you will come to a single cottage on the right. Opposite this, turn left into the field and walk down the right-hand side of it to the far end. There, turn right through a gate. Just before the road turn left into a bridleway. This takes you over a metalled road and past a barn, until, about ¾ mile later, you will go through a gate slightly left, into the Forestry Commission property.

Don't turn right immediately but continue up the ride for fifty yards and then turn right into a wide track. This takes you, more or less in a straight line, across several paths, until it brings you to a gate at the edge of the trees. Go through this and walk down the fenced track ahead of you to the further gate. On the way look out for a sight of Patching Church on the right. At the gate turn right, on to the path you started out on, and so back to the metalled road leading down into Patching.

16 *Parham Post – Amberley – North Stoke – Burpham – Wapham Down – Parham Post* 9 miles

General Description This very pleasant West Sussex walk starts at Parham Post, near Kithurst Hill, where there is good parking for cars. You go along the South Downs Way, overlooking Parham Park and Amberley Wild Brooks which are guarded by the mediaeval bishop's castle. You go down Amberley Mount, which Charles II rode up on his celebrated escape to France, and so to Amberley Station. After that you walk to North Stoke and along the river and through woods to Burpham, which is one of the most splendid secluded and picturesque villages in Sussex. Besides a notable twelfth-century church and a famous smuggling inn it boasts literary patronage, as John Ruskin stayed a lot at Peppering Farm. You return to the car up the Leper's Path, over a lovely stretch of open downland on paths that have scarcely changed since prehistoric times.

To get to Parham Post you will have to travel by car. There is a Southdown bus, Service 71, that runs from Arundel to Horsham along the B2139 at the base of the hill, but it is very infrequent, only once every two hours or so, and leaves you with a steep 1-mile climb to the top of the Downs. The turning to go up in the car is about 1 mile west of Storrington on the B2139 – regrettably it's unsignposted, but it is the only such turning for three miles on that road. Park at the end of the metalled road.

Maps The one-inch Sheet 182 (Brighton and Worthing) or the two-and-a-half-inch Sheets TQ 00 (Littlehampton) and TQ 01 (Storrington). See our map on page 43.

Stage One: Parham Post to Amberley Station—3 miles Walk westwards along the South Downs Way, with the Weald on your right. Bear right immediately after passing the clump of trees on Springhead Hill. After following the track for $1\frac{1}{2}$ miles, you will come to a gate at the top of a steep hill. You will see Downs Farm in front of you in the valley. Walk down the hill, and after a $\frac{1}{4}$ mile, bear slightly right over a stile and along a nice footpath close to the fence on the right. Shortly, you will go through a gate, and so on to a lane. Turn right, and after the bend, fork left down the hill. Turn left into the main road and walk under the railway bridge. Just past the Bridge Hotel turn left into the lane to North Stoke.

Stage Two: Amberley Station to Burpham—$2\frac{1}{2}$ miles On arriving in North Stoke turn left at a telephone box and follow the lane until it crosses the railway line. Just on the other side, you should turn half-right into a field. There's a path here, running downhill by the electricity poles, close to the fence on your right. At the bottom take the narrow signed footpath to the right, through the trees alongside the old loop of the river Arun. After a $\frac{1}{4}$ mile of this winding path, you will have crossed two narrow bridges. Shortly after the second of these, you will see a red-brick sluice gate across the drainage channel to your left. Cross this, and walk across the field, keeping close to the fence on your right. At the trees on the far side, go through a gateway and immediately bear right along the track up the hill. Go through a gate into a field, keeping on the track by the hedge. This leads to another gate, and into a well-defined track which takes you past Peppering Farm. At the junction of the lanes, walk down the one opposite you into Burpham.

Stage Three: Burpham to Parham Post—$3\frac{1}{2}$ miles Turn left just past the church into the village. Ignore the right turning down the hill to Wepham, but continue past the village store to a T-junction. Here turn right down the hill for 50 yards, and then left, on to a well-maintained track. This is the Leper's Path. Walk past the pumping station into a field and up the hill on the chalk track. Just on the crown of the hill you will come to some enclosed gallops. Cross them by going through the two small gates, go across the field on the other side, and cross the other half of the gallops in the same way as the first. Immediately turn left along a track, and after a few yards, bear half-right along a bridleway, close to the fence on the right. After going through a gate $\frac{1}{4}$ mile further on you will pass a wood on the right. Opposite the end of the wood you'll find a signpost indicating a faint path across a field, to the right. Take this, and at the fence on the other side of the field pick up a track coming from the wood and turn left on to it, with the fence on your right. Stay on this track for 1¼ miles – it takes you through gates up the valley back to your car.

---

17   *Arundel – Lyminster – Poling – Angmering – Goring*
      7½ miles

General Description One with a difference, in that it is all on the flat, though still exciting and interesting. It has been designed to be most useful for someone who has to use public transport – in this case the train, though you can travel by bus or car. From Arundel Station you have a superb view of the Castle and the Roman Catholic Cathedral. You walk to Lyminster, passing on the way a place of great antiquity – Knucker's Hole – which is a mere pond, but which is popularly supposed to be bottomless. According to the legend, a dragon lived in it in Saxon times, until it was slain by one John Pulk, whose tombstone is to be seen in Lyminster Church. From Lyminster you pass through the peaceful village of Poling, the affluent village of Angmering, go beside Highdown Hill, one of the most interesting archaeological hill sites in Sussex, to finish at Goring Station, happy I hope and ready for your next venture.

To get to Arundel I suggest is easiest by train. You will return from Goring Station. You can get there by bus, catching the limited-stop Service 10x which starts at Brighton. In this case, you return to Brighton by Service 31 from Goring. You can use a car, but you will have to park somewhere near Goring Station and catch a train out to Arundel.

Maps Either the one-inch Map, Sheet 182 (Brighton and Worthing) or the two-and-a-half-inch Sheet TQ 43 (Littlehampton). See our map on page 43.

Stage One: Arundel Station to Lyminster Church – 1½ miles
Cross over the railway bridge from the station exit, and after about 100 yards, turn right off the main road over a stile. Follow the telegraph poles over a field with trees in it and go through a gate into a larger field. At the end turn left on to a track through a gate,

now you immediately turn right. Walk by the hedge down to the bottom and over a fence. Here you pick up 'diverted footpath' signs by Broomhurst Farm. Follow these all the way to Lyminster Church, which you should be able to see in the distance. After you've passed through a bed of rushes you'll see the famous Knucker's Hole, which is by some watercress beds. At the church, turn left.

Stage Two: Lyminster Church to Angmering Church –
3 miles Walk straight on, to the road, the A284, and walk along it for 300 yards. At a sharp bend take the green path by a house in front of you. This leads you in a practically straight line across fields into Poling. Almost at the end of the hamlet take the foot-path signposted 'to the Church' and follow it through the church-yard and over the stile at the other end into a field. Now go through three gates: one in front of you, then one to the left, and finally one to the right. This leads you by a farm track with hedges either side into a field where you should cross over the wooden bridge on the right, and then over a stile.
In the distance you will see a row of houses. Make for the one by a tall tree on the left of the row, keeping a barn 150 yards to your right. You will pick up a path that will take you to these houses and to a stile. Walk down the road in front of you. It will lead you into the village by the church. Turn left.

Stage Three: Angmering Church to Goring Station –
3 miles Turn right into the High Street and follow this road out of the village for approximately half a mile to where it turns abruptly right. You keep straight on, by The Spotted Cow, along an avenue of trees. At a T-junction turn right into a bridlepath. Turn left and shortly, left again. Keep straight on this path for nearly a mile, ignoring all turnings until you go through a field. You should now be by an old chalk pit. Turn left through a hedge and immediately half-left on to a downland track. Walk to the new waterworks and turn right on to a path down past some green-houses to the main road. Cross the A259 and go down Ferring Lane. At the first bend take the path by the electricity pylons across the middle of the ploughed fields to a tarred path by the railway line. Turn left and walk to Goring Station.